T0156725

REMOVING THE GRAVECLOTHES

Removing hindrances in order
to pursue the Kingdom agenda

Bradley C. Johnson

iUniverse, Inc.
New York Bloomington

Copyright © 2009 by Bradley C. Johnson

All rights reserved. No part of this book may be used or reproduced by
any means, graphic, electronic, or mechanical, including photocopying,
recording, taping or by any information storage retrieval system
without the written permission of the publisher except in the case
of brief quotations embodied in critical articles and reviews.
The views expressed in this work are solely those of the author
and do not necessarily reflect the views of the publisher, and the
publisher hereby disclaims any responsibility for them.

iUniverse books may be ordered through booksellers or by contacting:

iUniverse
1663 Liberty Drive
Bloomington, IN 47403
www.iuniverse.com
1-800-Authors (1-800-288-4677)

Scripture quotations marked NLT are taken from the Holy Bible, New
Living Translation, copyright 1996, 2004. Used by permission of Tyndale
House Publishers, Inc., Wheaton, Illinois 60189. All rights reserved

Because of the dynamic nature of the Internet, any Web addresses or links
contained in this book may have changed since publication and may no longer be
valid. The views expressed in this work are solely those of the author and do not
necessarily reflect the views of the publisher, and the publisher hereby disclaims
any responsibility for them.

ISBN: 978-1-4401-2809-7 (sc)
ISBN: 978-1-4401-2810-3 (ebook)

Printed in the United States of America

iUniverse rev. date: 03/04/2009

Dedication

This book is dedicated to every man and woman that is struggling in this race called life. Not only those who are struggling with issues that can be seen, but those struggling with the issues in the dark. The issues that bog us down like depression, despair, and drama in a society that views Christianity as fashionable. This book is a tool for us in the body of Christ who are striving, and at times struggling, to become all that God is calling us to be. My hope is that as we journey together in this book that we will begin to identify some of the "graveclothes" that are hindering our destiny. Whether our issue is visible, invisible, psychological, or emotional, this book is a tool to encourage us that there is freedom and healing in Christ Jesus for any issue that we may face whether self imposed or demonically designed. God's will is that we would begin to believe what Jesus the Christ spoke, that He, indeed, came to set the captive free.

This book is also dedicated to the three special women than went home to be with the Lord within weeks of each other, during the process of this book. Mrs. Constance Rubama, my host mom, thanks for believing in me even before you knew me. Mrs. Eva Johnson, my grandma, my E.O., thank you for always listening to me even when I was a child. You made me feel like my thoughts and opinions were valid even when they didn't make sense. Finally, Mrs. Emily G. Beverly, my Nana, thank you for helping to rear me everyday of my life. You are my grandma/mom and life hasn't been the same since you left but I know that this side can't compare to the side your on now with Jesus. I hope that anything that I do in life would continue to reflect what you three ladies taught me and would make you proud of me. I love you always!!!

Table of Contents

INTRODUCTION

In John 11 the New Living Translation of The Bible accounts the resurrection of Lazarus from the dead as follows:

"A man named Lazarus was sick. He lived in Bethany with his sisters, Mary and Martha. This is the Mary who poured expensive perfume on the Lord's feet and wiped them with her hair. Her brother, Lazarus, was sick. So the two sisters sent a message to Jesus telling him, "Lord, the one you love is very sick."

But when Jesus heard about it he said, "Lazarus's sickness will not end in death. No, it is for the glory of God. I, the Son of God, will receive glory from this." Although Jesus loved Martha, Mary, and Lazarus, he stayed where he was for the next two days and did not go to them. Finally after two days, he said to his disciples, "Let's go to Judea again."

But his disciples objected. "Teacher," they said, "only a few days ago the Jewish leaders in Judea were trying to kill you. Are you going there again?"

"Jesus replied, " there are twelve hours of daylight every day. As long as it is light, people can walk safely. They can see because they have the light of this world. Only at night is there danger of stumbling because there is no light." Then he said, "Our friend Lazarus has fallen asleep, but now I will go and wake him up."

The disciples said, "Lord, if he is sleeping, that means he is getting better!" They thought Jesus meant Lazarus was having a good night's rest, but Jesus meant Lazarus had died.

Then he told them plainly, "Lazarus is dead. And for your sake, I am glad I wasn't there, because this will give you another opportunity to believe in me. Come, let's go see him."

Thomas, nicknamed the Twin, said to his fellow disciples, "Let's go, too- and die with Jesus."

When Jesus arrived at Bethany, he was told that Lazarus had already been in his grave for four days. Bethany was only a few miles down the road from Jerusalem, and many of the people had come to pay their respects and console Martha and Mary on their loss. When Martha got word that Jesus was coming, she went to meet him. But Mary stayed at home. Martha said to Jesus, "Lord, if you had been here, my brother would not have died. But even now I know that God will give you whatever you ask."

Jesus told her, "Your brother will rise again."

"Yes," Martha said, "when everyone else rises, on resurrection day."

Jesus told her, "I am the resurrection and the life. Those who believe in me, even though they die like everyone else, will live again. They are given eternal life for believing in me and will never perish. Do you believe this, Martha?"

"Yes, Lord," she told him. "I have always believed you are the Messiah, the Son of God, the one who has come into the world from God." Then she left him and returned to Mary. She called Mary aside from the mourners and told her, "The Teacher is here and wants to see you." So Mary immediately went to him.

Now Jesus had stayed outside the village, at the place where Martha met him. When the people who were at the house trying to console Mary saw her leave so hastily, they assumed she was going to Lazarus's grave to weep. So they followed her there. When Mary arrived and saw Jesus, she *fell down at his feet and said, "Lord, if you had been here, my brother would not have died."*

When Jesus saw her weeping and saw the other people wailing with her, he was moved with indignation and was deeply troubled. "Where have you put him?" he asked them.

They told him, "Lord, come and see." Then Jesus wept. The people who were standing nearby said, "See how much he loved him." But some said, "This man healed a blind man. Why couldn't he keep Lazarus from dying?"

And again Jesus was deeply troubled. Then they came to the grave. It was a cave with a stone rolled across its entrance. "Roll the stone aside," Jesus told them.

But Martha, the dead man's sister, said, "Lord, by now the smell will be terrible because he has been dead for four days."

Jesus responded, "Didn't I tell you that you will see God's glory if you believe?" So they rolled the stone aside. Then Jesus looked up to heaven and said, "Father, thank you for hearing me. You always hear me, but I said it out loud for the sake of all these people standing here, so they will believe you sent me." Then Jesus shouted, "Lazarus, come out!" And Lazarus came out, bound in graveclothes, his face wrapped in a headcloth. Jesus told them, "Unwrap him and let him go!"

Throughout my life, I have heard the story of the resurrection of Lazarus many times. Growing up in the Baptist denomination the story has always been packaged with the intent to exemplify the power of God to raise the dead and heal the sick. In many churches I have also heard this account being used as tool to teach the body that all powerful God has the awesome ability to raise the dead issues and dreams in our lives that many people see as being forever buried. Although these are both true revelations neither is quite the revelation that I received and will focus on in the preceding chapters.

In my walk with God I have often found that the issues that sometimes arise cannot easily be explained or pin pointed as the result of one specific event or occurrence in our lives. Because of this, I believe that looking at the resurrection and release of Lazarus can and will help the body of Christ to successfully identify and evaluate the hindrances in our lives that cause these potentially stagnating problems. These issues come in many shapes, sizes, and varieties and are as diverse as the colors of a Martha Stewart floral arrangement, yet they all lead to a parallelization in the Spirit.

God's Spirit has led me to focus in on a part of the story that is often read over or neglected as one of the major parts of the story. In John 11:43 we find Jesus standing in front of an open grave commanding a dead man to come forth out of a four day "hibernation" inside of a closed tomb. God's authoritative shout is given after affirming that Mary, Martha, and the other spectators would see the glory of God that day. This also happens after Jesus has just finished encouraging the faith of a weary and mourning Martha. As I read verse 43 for the billionth time, that recounts the dead man, Lazarus, coming forth out of the tomb, something in my Spirit clicked for the first time; the significance of the graveclothes!

Graveclothes can be defined as a shroud of fabric or garment that was used in that day to cover and protect the remains of the deceased after burial. These garments were often fabrics that had been rolled in or fragranced by oils and spices to cut down on the smell of a decaying corpse before and after burial. In this passage of scripture it appears that these garments were not only a form of coverage for the dead man, but a way in which to keep the limbs of the body secured near the torso of the deceased. The main fabric was accompanied by a head cloth that served a similar purpose for the skull.

As I began to study the story of Lazarus these graveclothes appear not only to be a form of preservation and protection for the deceased, but also a hindrance to his destiny. These graveclothes, which were designed to assure his protection in death, became a bondage that had to be removed in order for Lazarus to live life. God began to show me that the graveclothes of Lazarus are very significant to the Christian walk that each believer faces every day.

In the last year as I began to seek the Lord about this revelation, which I thought at the time was a sermon to be preached at a later date, God began to add more and more to this revelation. These additions far exceeded the depth of understanding that I believed could be gleaned from the story of Lazarus. Lazarus's resurrection mirrors the transformation of every believer from the old man into the new man in Christ. Yet Jesus' command for the graveclothes of Lazarus to be removed represents the change and journey of every progressive believer after conversion. I know many of you are thinking what journey? Isn't the whole plan for me to get saved and go to heaven? Shouldn't I be okay now? If this is your view point of this walk, then you are destined for a life of mediocrity and disappointment.

> *"Wherefore, my beloved, as ye have always obeyed, not as in my presence only, but no much more in my absence, work out your own salvation with fear and trembling."*
> — **Phil. 2:12 KJV**

When I decided in 2004 to truly give my life to the Lord Jesus Christ and truly surrender all, I was unaware of the journey that would take place, both in the Spirit and in the natural, to become the Man of God that I am destined to be. When first looking at salvation, the dreamy eyed convert may first believe that the Christian walk is one of fairy tales and church picnics. Others may believe that this walk is one where once conversion takes place, Jesus takes care of every problem, habit, and scenario in our lives. Both ideals are simply not true. I found myself more and more engulfed in a battle not for my eternal salvation, but for the establishment and progression of Christ like character in this temporary setting. I found myself in a fight to believe God in ways that I thought came with the territory of just being saved.

Growing up in church I always knew that God was real and that He loved me. Though I knew of Him, I never knew that a relationship with Him took more then just saying the sinner's prayer and going to church on every other Sunday. So naturally it was a shock to me in 2004 when I got serious about salvation. As I have lived these past three years as a man pursuing the will of God for my life, I have discovered that not every symptom of the struggles that I have had in my life left when Jesus became the Lord of my life. I do believe that when Jesus died on the cross for my sins that I was totally saved, delivered, prospered, and healed throughout every area of my life, but I do believe that it takes a building and sustaining of faith to live out the truth in areas that the devil had residence in prior to salvation. I believe that as Philippians 2:12 says that there are certain areas in our lives that not necessarily doom us to eternal damnation, but limit us in the expansion of the kingdom in the earth realm. As I journeyed to write this book these areas have become more and more prevalent in my own life.

I found out, at my conversion, that the devil did not and would not give up his ground with a Lazarus experience in my life. I came to Christ just as I was, as the old hymn says, and found that some of the same issues that I struggled with prior to salvation did not automatically disappear when I became a Christian. I know that you are probably quoting, "If any man be in Christ he is a new Creature" in your mind, but in the midst of our metamorphosis into the new creatures, we must learn how to walk as those creatures. No tadpole, when transforming into a frog, knows how to use their new legs right away. By the same revelation, most believers don't know how to walk as new creatures without personal guidance and direction from God through prayer, fasting, and the word of God. This transformation can be one of great trying, struggle, and discipline. But through these struggles we discover the Lazarus beneath the graveclothes.

Like Lazarus, God has called every blood bought believer back to life from the dead. He has done this by raising us by the power of His Spirit and calling us forth by the voice and sacrifice of His Son Jesus Christ. This calling forth guarantees new life and another chance to experience a relationship with Jesus. In John the twelfth chapter you find Jesus at the house of Lazarus enjoying a celebration dinner during the time right before Passover. This scene exemplifies the continuation of a relationship of both the raised and the raiser after the miraculous event. This celebration echoes to the believer today that our salvation and removal of graveclothes is designed to develop a deeper and more intimate relationship with Jesus Christ; such as shared between a frequent house guest and host. His sacrifice for us and His revealing of the graveclothes in our lives gives us the opportunity to fellowship with Him in a deeper and more intimate way. This deeper realm of fellowship reaffirms the fact that the resurrection is not temporary.

Be careful of the people that help to mend and repair the graveclothes that you seek to discard. These people, either knowingly or unknowingly, help us stay bound in attitudes, emotions, and garments that Jesus commands us to be loosed from. Often these people come in the forms of relationships or friendships with people who see our graveclothes and help in the process of convincing us that the garment is very fashionable, and that there is no need to disregard it because, we are in fact, fine the way we are. We should be very careful of both saints and sinners who "pat our demons." Often times the assignment of Satan is through people who come into our lives in the middle of our transformation and see that we are still not yet whole. The devil often uses these people, not to ambush us, but to just keep us from truly unwrapping. Like many women who zero in on a insecure man, these people use our graveclothes as their tool to manipulate, control, and even mold us into who they think we should be. Watch out for those who come on the scene who don't help the loosing process to accelerate, but slow it down. Always remember that most times, those who are bound by the same graveclothes that we are don't see the urgency of our unwrapping. Often times they can't even help in our loosing because their hands are also bound by the same things which prevent our movement. A handcuffed man can not offer us a key that he himself does not possess.

THE CRYPT OF DOUBT

"So, you see, it is impossible to please God without faith. Anyone who wants to come to him must believe that there is a God and that He rewards those who sincerely seek him." — **Hebrews 11:6 (NLT)**

Doubt is the believer's biggest enemy. Doubt is so handicapping to believers because it doesn't involve anyone else, including the devil, except for themselves. I often compare doubt to cancer that slowly spreads throughout the mind of the believer causing everything that it touches to slowly break down and deteriorate until nothing in that general area is able to function properly. In the book of Genesis doubt of the promises of God is what caused Adam and Eve to allow, and I do mean allow, the devil to deceive them. If you truly read and receive revelation from Genesis 3, Adam and Eve's main undoing was not entertaining the thoughts and notions of the devil; rather it was them doubting the character and words of God. The serpent's, the devil's, job was simply to present another option, but it was Adam and Eve's decision to give those options and words a place in their hearts and minds.

Doubt's bacteria, as it relates to graveclothes, is one of the most common areas that keep the body of Christ from walking in freedom. I have been led and empowered by Jesus Christ to help in the unwrapping of the believer from this bondage first because it is something that I am dealing with even as I write these very pages. What makes this piece of the grave so enticing is its subtlety. Doubt doesn't have to aggressively take you over, or rapidly zap your faith; all it has to do is find a place and a welcoming option to reside. The Bible tells us in Ephesians 4:27 "Neither give place to the devil."(KJV) because of the emphasis on the believers participation in allowing the devil, in this case the spirit of doubt, to be able to live in and bind their very being.

It doesn't take much to be moved out of your place of faith. Often times we believe that we are securely standing in a place of faith because when the small problems of life come our way, like a cell phone bill or gas, we are not moved. But the question that has often been offered in my spirit is what do we do when the real scenarios hit the fan and we are provoked, sometimes even by God, out of our comfort zone. These problems often time are not monetary because in many situations those problems can be solved by man's methods. But how do we stand in situations that involve a need for healing, forgiveness, a covering of love, or even salvation. I have often found that we stand in faith in theory but not in practice. Many believers have often stood in faith for the healing of another saint until the sickness that they "bound" and "rebuked" pays a visit to their front door. What will the righteous do? As the arms and legs of Christ it is our responsibility to stand in faith according to the word despite a change in the climate or situation. The word is the word is the word.

I have often had to reevaluate my own place of faith. God began to bring about questions in my spirit as I journeyed to right this book. Do you really believe me, says the Lord? Do you really trust My Word? Do you really believe, not partially but entirely, what I have spoken? Do you believe that from start to finish I am still the same? Many believers wouldn't dare say that they believed one part of the Bible but doubted the other. Or even dare to say that there were whole parts of the word of God that they have omitted from their lives because they found it too hard to not doubt. These are critical hits out on the Christians that keep us saved yet not whole. If we are ever to walk out the true destiny that God has for us, then we must develop a faith that says God I want all of you or nothing. If your word says healing from lepercy, then I believe that there is healing from

AIDS. If you are the same God that delivered a man from a tormenting demon who lived in a graveyard (Luke 8:27-33), then He can command every homosexual and lesbian spirit to loose the struggling saints and the unsaved. If God is the God whom laid down His life and then picked it up three days later and laid His graveclothes to the side, then surely my issue, my graveclothes, my affliction, has got to let me go!

I believe that there is a special hit out on the men of the body of Christ. As I stated before, I have grown up in the church all my life and have seen many men with spiritual afflictions, including myself, that become potentially crippling to their destiny. Because I am an African American Christian man, I would like to take the time to focus in on this particular demographic. Normally in the African American church you find four types of men. The man who's whole masculinity is tied up in sports and how much of a whore he was before he got saved, the angry soldier who's so frustrated with the pressures of life and family that he comes just to keep from exploding, the emasculated man who has been forced, by his wife, to be the submissive and timid man in his own home, and the homosexual who often times is the most vocal in the church setting, yet is, most times, totally outside of the will and character of God.

All four of these men are facing the same weight of doubt. In a society who only gives men, especially black men, a small variety of roles to play, these men have lost their identity and begin to doubt the plans and identity of God. All these men at one point or another in their lives have doubted and lost who God created them to be because of the temporal circumstance that they once found themselves in. The journey out of doubt for men is often one that is seen as either private or not necessary by most of society, sadly the church, and even the women who are supposed to love us. So many men are crying out in the dark to know "Who am I?" because somewhere along the way doubt about their masculinity, vulnerability, likability, or even sexuality caused them to lose their way and spiral off into an alter ego. He's alive yet still not recognizable through the graveclothes.

Who am I? This is the question that all people ask themselves from time to time, yet I venture to say that most of us, especially men don't know. Jeremiah 1:5-7 says, "Before I formed thee in the belly I knew thee; and before thou camest forth out of the womb I sanctified thee, and I ordained thee a prophet unto the nations. Then said I, Ah, Lord God! Behold, I cannot speak, for I am a child. But the Lord said unto me, Say not, I am a child: for thou shalt go to all that I shall send thee, and whatsoever I command thee thou shalt speak" (KJV). This verse of scripture alludes to the fact that there is an identity before our lives begin that God has for us to walk out in the flesh. This includes our personality, make up, and destiny. The problem with most believers, especially men, is that we don't spend enough time with God, or truly in our hearts do not believer that He knew what He was doing when He created us. This is a harsh blow to most of our egos but it's true none the less. To venture into most of our minds, we would find a mentality that boasts that we shaped our own image, and that God, much like the womb, was just how we got here. How doubt operates in this arena is to cause us to begin to believe that the truth of who we are is totally up to us thereby nullifying the need for or connection to God. Many atheists, Unitarians, and sadly even some Christians view God as a source that put us here to do our own thing. When we begin to believe, at any point in our lives, that I'm here to do my own will, even if we package it in a Godly scenario of free will, we open ourselves up for deception and further grave clothes to not only bind our bodies, but our minds.

As a Christian man, doubt has often tried to attack and harass me out of the will of God. I grew up being primarily raised by my mother. My parents got divorced when I was four and both I and my brother stayed with my mother. During my whole life my father has also always been a constant part of my life. Because of my rearing I often was the victim of ridicule by other people because I wasn't the macho dude. Like most young guys who weren't into a lot of sports, besides basketball, I was called gay and punk and feminine. This label was something that I found, though not as severe, would attempt to follow me and plague me through my whole teenage and young adult life. Growing up I never looked at myself as being different from any of the other fellows, I just didn't like stupid stuff and nonsense; coincidentally, most of the time that left me playing with the girls. Being reared by my mother, that didn't bother me because I saw people as people, and if the girls were trying do what I wanted to do and go where I wanted to go, then I had no problem being the only dude in the group. Ironically, that scenario is what helped me get a lot of my girlfriends in the early days. Yet I find as I look back now I can see how the seeds of doubt attempted to destroy my faith in myself and in what God called me to be. Never in my life have I ever had any type of encounter, relationship, or flirtation with anyone of the same sex, but I have, during my teenage and early adult years, had periods of time when I was plagued by demonic spirits, sometimes in the forms of real people, that spoke to my mind to try to drive me in that direction. I say this not out of some type of pity, but I believe that someone reading this will get delivered through the testimony.

These spirits would come in seasons. They would plague my mind and even sometimes my dreams telling me that I wasn't going to become the man that God called me to be and that I was on my way out of the faith. They told me that no woman would ever love me, I was ugly, and that I would either die living a homosexual lifestyle or alone. They tried to convince me, even through day time television, that things like that weren't that bad and that it was a part of my, now I know a demonic, destiny. As these attacks came God still was speaking as well, letting me know that the things that I was hearing in my mind and dreams was not Him and not His will for my life, and that the people's and the demon's words would not prosper. These things were designed to pull me out of a place of faith. Never forget that the first thing that the devil will try to do, if you haven't truly opened yourself up to his influence, is try to attack your mind to make you open yourself up yourself. Through my trial and experience one thing that I never did was truly give the devil place. I chose (Daniel 1:8) whose side I was on. I'm not saying that it was always easy but I am a living testimony that God will deliver you through the blood of Jesus Christ and keep you if you truly want to be kept. In the midst of my dilemma as the doubt and confusion came God gave me the revelation of His word. Because I truly wanted to be kept by the most High I began to feast on His word that showed me who I was in Him. This allowed me to know who God intended me to be before He created me. Through the years and before I truly got saved, I had heard in my mind, in my dreams, and through other people who the enemy said that I was. It was finally time for me to hear what the Creator of me said that I was. Jeremiah 29:11 says, "For I know the thoughts that I think toward you, saith the Lord, thoughts of peace, and not of evil, to give you an expected in." That's where a lot of us have missed it, we have heard and believed what everybody else has said we were. Yet we give up because we say that we can't and won't truly believe who Jehovah Mephalti (the Lord our deliverer) says that we are. The Bible clearly lets us know that without a vision the people perish which includes us. If we don't tap into the vision or plan that God has for our lives then, even if we don't miss heaven, parts of our destinies and purpose in the earth will perish from our lives and callings.

A change in my thinking and faith level didn't happen over night. To walk out of the graveclothes of doubt in any area of your life takes discipline and dedication; especially in the area of how you see yourself. The statement of me getting in God's word to allow Him to show me me was a process of walking out Romans 12:1-2 (KJV).

"I beseech therefore bretheren, by the mercies of God, that ye present your bodies a living sacrifice, holy, acceptable

*unto God, which is your reasonable service. And be not conformed to this world: but **be ye transformed by the renewing of your mind**, that ye may prove what is that good, and acceptable, and perfect, will of God."*

Not only has God called believers to memorize the word but we must walk it out everyday of our lives, not to seem spiritual, but because this word is the deliverance and salvation of our very souls. When I speak of this, my struggle and journey out of doubt, I write from the perspective of someone who has confessed the Lord Jesus Christ as Lord, Savior, and Master of my life and because of that has been delivered from every spirit that the Lord has revealed to me whether perversion, lust, harassing spirits trying to push me into homosexuality, or doubt. I want to make this clear. Only when you have decided to accept Christ and are at a place of faith that you believe that when you accepted Him that He has totally delivered you, saved you, healed you, and prospered you, can you walk out of the place of doubt in your identity. Without security in Christ, then the spirit of doubt and any other spirit has the right to harass you, attack you, bind you, and possess you. Jesus has come and He has set the captive free (Luke 4:18).The blood of Jesus is a powerful thing.

God has called me, even though I don't fully know why, to assist in the unwrapping process of the saints. In John 11:45 after Jesus raised Lazarus from the dead with the shout of His voice He commanded the saints and mourners that were standing around to loose him and let him go. We must share in the responsibility of the body to help those still entangled in graveclothes to be unwrapped. Many of the problems that we have with the saints would be eliminated if we, in love and the Spirit's leading, would help in their unwrapping. As Lazarus pushed forth toward Christ I can imagine with every step, or hop, the bystanders grabbing at a piece of cloth until Lazarus was finally free and falling at the feet of Jesus.

Walking in deliverance and freedom takes hard work. God never promised us that we would skip through the daisies in our daily life, but He did promise us peace, joy, assurance, and protection in Him. As we begin to unwrap doubt, along with any other graveclothes, in our life, we must realize that we will have to do the things in front while God is moving in the background doing the extreme warfare. In the story of Lazarus, Jesus purposely commanded the bystanders to do something. He could have commanded the graveclothes to fall off, but He said you who say you are spiritual; you, who are redeemed; you, who have been restored; loose him and let him go. Zachariah 3:3-4 further explains this when God told the angels that stood before Him with Joshua to remove the filthy raiments that Joshua was wearing because He had new clothes for him to wear. God helps us as we help ourselves.

Brothers I want to leave you with one important thing in this chapter. Only when you begin to peel off the layers of false identity that you have built up over the years through what television, your parents, saved or unsaved, your coaches, rap music, or even your spouses have told you can you truly find the man that God created you to be. There are so many of us who have woman and society telling us, "stand up and be a man;" yet there are so many of us I hear crying in the Spirit, tell me how because no one ever taught me. Doubt in God and doubt in ourselves have left us confused, alone, and in a place of just feeling our way in and out of the will of God. Those of you who are reading this as saved men please understand this, the identity of David, Jeremiah, Paul, Moses, and many other great men in the Bible was never ever ever determined or built on their wealth, their looks, their wives, sports, or their power to front. Their identity was birthed out of their ability to hear and obey God, and then walk out the plan that they heard with a pure heart and a willing spirit. As we raise our sons and our grandsons please remember that their identities have been planned by God and we must grasp the plan of God for them as an individual and steer them into their purpose. A man that's truly walking out there purpose leaves no place for doubt to live.

EVERY SEED SOWN

"Be not deceived; God is not mocked: for whatsoever a man soweth, that shall he also reap. For he that soweth to his flesh shall reap of corruption; but he that soweth to the Spirit shall reap of the Spirit life everlasting." — **Galatians 6: 7-8**

Some of it is your fault. I know that this is hard to believe and even harder to admit but you cause some of your graveclothes. You may be ready to donate this book to someone else that you may believe caused their own problems, but first know that you caused some of your own too. When I first began to review my life and wonder why so many attacks were occurring on my mind, I began to reflect on my past and critique the story. Based upon the Word of God I have found that everything blossoms from a seed that is planted. Whether it is trees, fruit, plants, us, or even the Word of God, they are all a reproduction of a spermatic act. Paul wrote to the church of Corinth and explained that even with the Word, one man plants, another man waters, but it's God who gives the increase. As I seek to explain whether good or bad the seeds that are planted in us have been planted, watered, and either the most High God or us cooperating with the devil has caused the increase.

In looking back on my life God began to take me back to past experience that planted the seeds that become graveclothes in my life. Before I write anymore I want to give you all a little disclaimer. Some of the people that I am about to discuss in relations to seeds planted were either unsaved or ignorant to the fact at that time that they were helping in the planting of seeds in by soulish and fleshly realms. I no longer hold them accountable or responsible because of the fact that I am a Christian now and through the Word of God have found the weed killer for every ungodly seed. I have recovered.

One of the major seeds, that grew into graveclothes, in my life, was lust. I can remember never really seeing true pornography in my life until I got to college. I think that during that time my best friend from back home and I were the only two of our friends that were still virgins. We both began to hangout with the same crew and most of the guys in the group were pornography addicts. These guys had up to 300 porno movies on their computers between them. No one ever forced me to watch anything, but not truly being saved and wanting to fit in, I opened my eye gate (1John 2:16) to the seed of pornography. During this time I could feel God pulling on me but I was already struggling with masturbation and lust. The introduction of pornography simply accelerated the process. This world opened my flesh to dimension of lust that I never new before. I began to watch pornography with them on a regular basis. This opened my mind to new places of perversion of sexual sin and perversion that I would have never known had I not exposed myself to it. One thing that I have discovered about most demonic spirits, but especially lust, is that it is never satisfied with a onetime scenario. It will always push to new levels of decay. As I thought about it, I now believe that watching pornography was a watering of the seeds that were planted through my life by older males in my life through not only their words about women and what I should be doing with them, but also by the sexual movies that I was allowed to watch with them without my mother's knowledge. Now as I look back, even some movies that are shown as rated R in movie theaters plant seeds in the minds of our youth.

The seeds that were planted helped in the binding process as I truly began to walk with God. As I stepped into the body of Christ I found myself still struggling with masturbation and lust because of seeds that had been planted through my eye gate. Because I opened myself up for the seeds to planted, it gave the devil a door to bind my mind. Those images, much like film, were burned into to my mind, my soulish realm, and could and did pop at any time. The more I watched the more they would pop up when I was awake, in church, in my word, or most normally in my dreams. Now I know that most men are saying that this is natural. I beg to differ. These things are natural in the sense that they are carnal, detrimental, and handicapping to our spiritual selves. God would never have commanded us in Romans 12:1-2 to renew our minds if we were meant to continually feed and think on these things. Yes, it is true that most men have wet dreams at physical maturity, but I don't believe that it is the will of God for us to need anything else besides our imaginations, while were asleep, to create those scenarios. The Bible tells us that as believers we are supposed to be led by our spirits in conjunction with the Holy Ghost not by our flesh. Anything that dominates our every day thinking and life, besides the Word of God is demonic in nature and unprofitable for the believer. Even at the age that I am now I very rarely have wet dreams because of the fact that I try to make sure that the most of what goes before my eyes is edifying to my spiritual man, the true me. Every believer, keep in mind whatsoever you sow to is going to grow. If you are like many believers who are wrapped up in the graveclothes of lust, if you continue to watch, listen to, and speak about lustful and sexual things you are only feeding the weed that is keeping the true you from coming forth. These seeds open the doors to other types of graveclothes to bind you.

Hear me and hear me well; I believe that pornography is demonically designed to draw you deeper and deeper into perversion in your life. I believe that any man who has become consumed or regularly watches pornography will eventually move on to homosexuality. The devil mission is to steal, kill, and destroy. He ultimately wants your soul. I have talked with other Christians who have relayed to me that as a result of the pornography that they watched, they had to begin to cast down thoughts of homosexuality in their everyday life. Like most people who have had so much premarital sex that they move on to other things because that no longer is enough, many pornography watchers begin to forget who they are most observing in the movies. The more they watch, the more sexual lines become blurred and they begin to wonder, am I looking at the woman or the man in the movie? During my teenage and early adult life, I have seen some crazy things on the television and internet. Just to illustrate how perverted and progressive lust is, during the time period when I was watching pornography I have seen people having sex with animals and with trees in a movie. Now even though these images did nothing for me sexually, for many these images are an entrance into a whole new level of perversion. Parents watch your children. Others might say that you are being overprotective or to spiritual, but I would rather you have done everything that the Word has told you to do to protect your children's innocence even if they still choose to do the wrong thing, than for you to allow them to be exposed to too much and then know that you share the blame in them destroying or delaying their destiny.

Other seeds grew in my life through music. In my life I have always been a lover of all kinds of music with maybe the exception of heavy metal. I come from a very musical family and have a gifting and anointing for music myself. It now makes since to why this would be a crafty way for the devil to get a message to me. Through most of my life I mostly stuck with the genres of R&B and hip-hop. During my generation we had singers like Mary J. Blige, Mariah Carey, Carl Thomas, 112, Total, Faith Evans, Monica, and Brandy to name a few. We had rappers like Nas, Jay-Z, Biggie, LL, Lil' Kim, Foxy Brown, and The Firm too. I was a fan of most of these people. I would say during my lifetime is when music changed the most and the lyrical content became increasingly sexual, violent, and graphic in nature. The Bible tells us that we can have what we say, and truly that includes the things that we sing as well. I was like many young people who didn't see the connection at first. God had to reveal to me that over the years as I idolized and listened to these people and sang there lyrics that I was helping in my own binding process. As I sang the words to a lot of their songs I was receiving their philosophy in my own life and slowly but surely my mentality was changing more in the direction of carnality than spiritually.

The lyrics of most of the music I was listening to helped to strengthen the graveclothes. Galatians 6 tells us that whatsoever we sow to is what we will reap of, and that's what happens often times with the music that we sing and listen to. Many of the issues in my life that have tried to bind me even in salvation are a direct result of the things that I exposed myself to then. Issues like lust and perversion can be traced back to many lyrics I used to sing and listen to by the Lil' Kims and Foxy Browns of the rap world. Issues of violence and rage that I battled can be linked to the Biggies and Nas' as well. Many people may not agree with this link but the Word of God clearly states that what ever you sow to is going to grow. I'm not attacking the artist in this instance but the lyrical content that produces spiritual consequences. I spent years listening to these people and having my mind and ideology shaped by what I saw them say and do. I know many of you are probably saying, "That's not me, I have my own mind and I like the beat," but tell me how many of you all's whole wardrobe is filled with what you saw on BET. Also how many of us when we listen to a lot of the artist that we listen to only hear the beat and never learn the words to the song? If that is your truth, then start buying the instrumentals and see how long you believe it's still just the beat. I'm just trying to inform all of us that what ever we sow to is going to grow. The graveclothes will continue to constrict us and get stronger as long as we help them. Finally I want to share with you the revelation that God gave me. I sometimes flip to BET just to see how far music has gone in the wrong direction and to see how the creativity has so greatly diminished over the past decade. Even though I sometimes do that God has instructed me not to buy or listen to secular music under my control, keep in mind that I can't control what others are playing around me. I am not saying that if you are a Christian that you are going to hell if you listen to secular music, but this is what God has given me for my life. Paul tells us in 1 Cor. 6:12 "All things are lawful unto me, but all things are not expedient: all things are lawful for me, but I will not be brought under the power of any." For those of you who may be music artist, like me, or aspiring music artist, this may be something that you want to pay close attention to. I can't explain it but there is something about being a musician that causes you to feel the music. When I was listening to secular music, there were times that I felt the music so deeply that I thought it was me. In the words of today's youth, I would get caught up! Maybe it is because I am a songwriter, but often times I would find myself caught by the lyrics of a song and feel the pain, hurt, anger, and depression of the artist singing it. Even though this might not be wrong for everyone, I was definitely brought under the power of the music. My emotions, feelings, mindset, and mood could be changed by hearing one song. God had to take it away. I want to only be moved by the Spirit of God. Once again this might not be wrong or addictive for you as a believer but I know for this season in my life, buying a R&B artist's latest project is not expedient. Maybe it will change once I'm married.

I found myself being plagued by thoughts and imaginations as I walked as a Christian that I really thought had no impact on me. Things that I once thought was just lyrics or music became a tool that would pop in my mind at the most inopportune times. I could be trying to worship God and R. Kelly's "Down Low" would come to my mind. Other times I would be trying to carry on a saved relationship with a young lady and Nas' "K-I-S-S-I-N-G" would come to my mind. Despite what other people might admit these things influence our perspective on life situations; Faith comes by hearing. You begin to believe what you hear all the time. Anybody that might dispute that must answer one question for me. If you are one of those people who says, "you just didn't have any mind of your own, I'm strong" tell me this how come you claim to be such a individual and free thinker, yet everyday you dress like, talk like, spit game like, and even walk down the street quoting the lyrics of 50 Cent and Jay-Z. Even in the midst of a conversation you say, "Well like my man 50 say" etc, etc. These statements become truer in our lives than the Word of God. We remember more of 50's, Nas's, Beyonce's, and Justin Timberlake's lyrics than we do scriptures from The Bible. So tell me without your Sword (Ephesians 6) what else do you have to go by then what you're feeding yourself. The seeds have been planted.

Also at times I have questioned God as to why and, in all realness, sometimes I did, want to go back to some of the artist that weren't necessarily helping, as I saw it, to strengthened my graveclothes; people like Faith Evans, Mary J. Blige, Lauryn Hill, and Carl Thomas. I would rationalize in my head about how their lyrics weren't contrary to the Word and how they were Christians, but God stopped me with one sentence, "They're not helping in the renewing process." It was true that these artists weren't necessarily hurting me but at the same time they weren't helping either. We are told in Romans 12:1-2 to present our bodies to God and to be transformed by the renewing of our minds, and realistically some things just don't help that to happen. Hebrews 12:1 admonishes us to lay aside every weight that so easily besets us and to run with endurance (NLT) the race that God has set before us. This means that there are certain things that may not be out rightly helping to bind us, but they are also not doing anything to help us in the unwrapping process. I finally had to ask myself this question. Would I prefer to be entertained or unwrapped?

STIFLED BY THE PAST

> *"but this one thing I do, forgetting those things which are behind, and reaching forth unto those things which are before, I press toward the mark for the prize of the high calling of God in Christ Jesus."* — **(Philippians 3:13-14)**

One of the hardest obstacles to overcome is our past. Not because it may determine our future, but because it takes an admittance of the fact that at one time we were in that place, in that situation, and at that time, and most painfully, we were that person. The past has a way of sneaking up on you when you most believe that it is miles behind. Many believers have been crippled and suffocated by the fear that one day their past would some how come up behind them. Often times I believe that believers become complacent not because they actually see their past coming up behind them, but because of the possibility that it one day might. Paul admonishes us to follow his example to forget those things which are behind us and press toward what is ahead, but the trouble is many believers don't really know how. In the unwrapping process from unusable bandages of past hurt, past sins, and past issues we must get over the monster that we once called ourselves. If we are to be unwrapped into destiny we must realize that the blood of Jesus killed the past and drowned it in the see of forgetfulness, and the only way that it will appear again is if we rebuild it in our present and future.

When examining the past, an interesting person in the Word of God to look at is Paul. Most of us know Paul as the man of God who the Holy Spirit moved upon to write two thirds of the New Testament, but this move of God in Paul's life only came after the graveclothes of Saul fell off. Acts the eighth and ninth chapter narrate the story of Saul's conversion into Paul. Saul was a Pharisee who brutally persecuted the church. He was responsible and took delight in seeing Christians brutally murdered and imprisoned for speaking of this Jesus that Saul did not know. In Acts 9 you see the account of Saul meeting Jesus on the road to Damascus and having an experience that forever changed his life. After Saul met the Lord Jesus his name and destiny was forever changed. In later chapters of the book of Acts you find the other Apostles having trouble believing in the conversion of Paul because of the time frame and evidence of who he once was. This skepticism rings true in many believers lives today. Often times both Christians and non Christians have trouble believing that we are truly changed because they knew us before we met Jesus. They saw our antics and remember our speech so it becomes hard for them to truly believe that a sudden change has come upon us. One difference between Paul and many of us is that Paul proved his change by his fruit not by his words. In reality Paul didn't have to prove to the other Apostles that he had truly been changed by the power of God, but because of the fact that he had made a commitment to follow God and the direction of the Holy Spirit, his life told them of his change. Many believers are saying I have been changed, yet our lives show that we still are wrapped by our past. We use the famous line, "ain't nobody perfect," but like Paul, if we have truly been changed into a new creature and have found the Lord Jesus, then the remnant of a transformation will be seen because our hearts would be seeking after God. Changes always produce fruit. We can never be truly free from our graveclothes until we begin to see Jesus as bigger than any problem we face. If it's cancer, Jesus is bigger. If it's AIDS, Jesus is bigger. If its lesbianism or homosexuality, Jesus is bigger. If it's lust, Jesus is bigger. If its financial, Jesus is still bigger. No matter what our graveclothe is Jesus is still big enough to bring us over and out of it.

Often times our transformation is bogged down by our perception of how others see our change. I believe Paul's change was so noticeable, not because he sought to look changed before man, but because he was changed in the eye sight of God. As I stated before, I have had many people call me many things in my childhood that it has taken me many years to receive healing for. I have been called punk, sissy, faggot, little girl, stupid, dumb, ugly, fat, etc. in my past, and even after coming to Christ these names have haunted me from the catacombs of my past. My graveclothes of the past was not that I believed that I wasn't transformed by the power of the resurrection of Jesus, but that no matter what, others, even if they didn't say it, still saw me the way that the devil saw me. Even after coming to Christ I tried so hard to prove that I wasn't those things that I ran myself physically and emotionally ragged. So many of us try so hard to prove the "them" in our past wrong, that we forget to just be from our spirit. John 4:24 says that God is a Spirit and they that worship Him, must worship Him in spirit and in truth. Whether you realize it or not you are a spirit being. Your flesh, blood, and tissue will one day be gone and you will see yourself in a spiritual form if you meet God before the rapture. God tells us in Jeremiah 1 that He knew us before we were formed in our mother's womb. Which alludes to the fact that there is certain things that God saw and placed in you spirit that you may not see yet but are manifesting themselves in your life even now. When we come to Christ we become alive in a spirits and reconnected to God. We gain eternal life by our spirit (John 3:16). I, like so many other believers, became so worried about people seeing traces of my past in me or seeing me the way that some others, even though it was untrue, had once seen and called me, that I had forgot that newness would flow out of me automatically because I had truly met Jesus. See the change that happened in you, man or woman of God, doesn't happen in you because of something that you look like it, happens because you have truly met Jesus Christ.

Once you have truly met Him and get to grow intimately with Him, changes are produced because you're becoming like Him. I don't have to prove that I'm changed by forcing myself to do something outwardly. I'm changed because like Paul, after I met Jesus I chose to follow Him and my focus is on Him, and not on proving another wrong. This is what led others to see a change in me. The graveclothes had to fall off because others opinions of me began to matter less and less, but pleasing God became more and more important. As my heart began to be transformed by His word, my life began to be transformed by His promises. It no longer was the thoughts that I have to do this to prove this one or that one wrong. It became, I do this to prove the Lord Jesus right. Right in the sense that I am who He says I am, right in the sense that I am more than a conqueror, right in the sense that every tongue the rises up against me in judgment shall be condemned, right in the sense that I am fearfully and wonderfully made, right in the sense that I am a new creature in Christ, right in the sense that I will believe the report of the Lord, and right in the sense that He spoiled principalities and powers and made a show of them openly. Oh hallelujah to know that I am who God says I am and my past doesn't determine my present or future!! I don't have to prove it; all I have to do is live. Lazarus past said that he was dead stinking in his grave, but it was Jesus who said the largest part of his story was yet to be written. Before Lazarus's first death there was not much written in the Bible about him, but it was his main encounter with Jesus that truly rewrote his future. One encounter with Jesus changed both the story of his past and his future. No longer was he Lazarus the dead man, Lazarus Mary's brother, or Lazarus Martha's brother; he became Lazarus the man that Jesus gave new life to with the shout of His voice and Lazarus, forever changed by the unwrapping by the bretheren. Brother/sister I will say to you this hour to remember that your past will not come back if you only allow yourself to be truly transformed. Though the devil may try to tempt you or even send someone to remember your headstone, like Jesus, the body that they are looking for no longer occupies this space. Jesus has called you by your name and commanded your past to loose you and let you go. So when they see you and try to call you by the dead man/woman's name have assurance in your spirit that you have been given a new identity in Christ. I want to leave you in this chapter with a powerful quote from a woman of God that visited my Church, "I may have done what you said I did, but I am not who you say I am."

THE DECAY OF REBELLION

"Now's your opportunity!" David's men whispered to him. "Today is the day the Lord was talking about when he said, 'I will certainly put Saul into your power, to do with as you wish.'" Then David crept forward and cut off a piece of Saul's robe. But then David's conscience began bothering him because he had cut Saul's robe. "The Lord knows I shouldn't have done it," he said to his men. "It is a serious thing to attack the Lord's anointed one, for the Lord himself has chosen him." So David sharply rebuked his men and did not let them kill Saul. After Saul had left the cave and gone on his way, David came out and shouted after him, "My lord the king!" And when Saul looked around, David bowed low before him." — **I Samuel 24:4-8 (NLT)**

Being in rebellion is one of the most deadly and quickest ways to lose the favor of God. The graveclothes of rebellion has the potential to overlay other grave clothes in the believer's life, potentially stopping the unwrapping process all together. You see there are certain graveclothes that if not carefully unwrapped could halt our march toward freedom all together. Rebellion is definitely one of these major items. Actually rebellion has a way of hastening the death and decaying, both spiritually and naturally, in our lives. Have you ever noticed that most people that live their whole lives by their own rules still never find happiness and a sense of peace?

Let us focus on our focal scripture to examine a man who had every right to be rebellious yet found favor with God because of his heart for leadership. In the story of David and King Saul, Saul lost his right as king due to rebellion and jealousy directed toward God and toward a shepherd named David. Saul rebelled against God in I Sam. 28, after receiving the word that his reign as king would soon be over, by consulting with a witch about the fate of the kingdom after God had forbidden His chosen people Israel to consort with psychics and mediums. Saul's rebellion against God was a result of his jealousy of David, for he feared that David would soon usurp power of the nation from Him. To back track, Saul's first rebellion against the Lord occurred in I Sam. 13 when instead of waiting for the priest Samuel to offer the burnt offering unto the Lord, Saul being disturbed by the loss of his troops at the hands of the Philistines, offered the burnt offering to the Lord minutes before Samuel arrived. This one impatient choice caused Saul to lose the throne. The seed of rebellion that found a place in Saul's heart that day plagued him until it caused hi death in later chapters. The spirit of rebellion is and has always been demonically designed to push the believer out of the will of God and thereby out of their destiny.

Romans 13:1-2 (NLT) says, "Obey the government, for God is the one who put it there. All governments have been placed in power by God. So those who refuse to obey the laws of the land are refusing to obey God, and punishment will follow." This is a topic that many believers struggle with. Those of us who have grown to a place of maturity find it easy to submit to our pastors, bishops, and church leaders, but not our bosses, judges, and officials. Why? I believe that it is a combination of experiences, paranoia's, and attitudes that make it hard for even believers to totally submit, but it is the spirit of rebellion that lays as one of the roots of this behavior. I believe that this spirit, or graveclothe, of rebellion is so enticing to even Christians because it appeals to a seed that was sown into our flesh back in the garden. Since the conversation of Eve with the serpent where the first man and woman entertained the idea of becoming like God, mankind has struggled with the pride of the flesh, rooted in rebellion, to control their own destiny. The unsaved have fought, to no avail, against society's standards to prove that, as many say, "I do what I want to do and you can't tell me what to do." This

seed uses mankind's limited knowledge to its advantage to blind
the minds (I Tim. 4:2) of man while they think they are free.
How does this apply to the Christians? Many Christians have
received the revelation, previously discussed, about submission
to our spiritual authorities, but still deal with the old nature in
the realm of the secular work world. Often times because of our
spirit man we find it more and more easy to submit to those that
live upright, but those who we serve under that are not in the
kingdom are often times seen as unworthy to be over us by many
believers. I know that many of you are saying that that's not you,
but more than likely we all have had a supervisor that was, to be
generous, not the most likable person. In being under them we
said, did, and didn't do something that we should have or could
have because of how we felt about them. Even though this was
something that we should have or could have because of how
we felt about them. Even though this was something that seems
so small in our heart we gave place to rebellion. Anybody that
God puts over us in any capacity is supposed to he honored and
obeyed by us as believers as long as they are not asking us to do
things contrary to the Word. Even then we are commanded not
to speak negatively or gossip about them, but to pray for them
and hear the voice of God for the next action we should take.
Anytime that we don't comply we are not getting back at them,
we are putting ourselves in a position to block the blessings and
favor of God in our own lives. So am I saying that if your boss
is a total jerk and rude you have to honor them? Yes, because we
are honoring the position that they are in since it was ordained
of God. In the story of David, he had the opportunity to kill
Saul and didn't, not because Saul was so great, but because of the
position in God he represented. Saul was crazy but David left it
up to God to take care of him, something that most of us don't
trust God enough to do. One of the reasons that many of us
can't submit is because we ultimately don't trust God to handle
other people or that He knew what He was doing when He put
the person over us that He has chosen. It really boil down to us

needing to trust God enough to work even through those people we don't understand to, like David, bring us into kingship.

David's relationship with Saul also brought about the revelation that submitting to authority doesn't always mean agreeing with everything that those in leadership do or say. I know that this is contrary to church etiquette and man made doctrine, but it is the truth. Over the course of my salvation I have seen so many people act as if they didn't agree with Pastorial or other leadership that it was some type of sin, when according to scripture it's not. In the life of David the Bible suggest that there were many differences in the thought patterns and personalities of himself and Saul, yet David still submitted to him. I have seen countless church members and other leaders agree with leaders and religious officials on ideologies and view points even when those philosophies were both ethically wrong and contrary to the Word of God. I have seen men and women of God make a false statement, and have those under their leadership agree whole heartedly with them even when they were wrong. For a long time I couldn't understand why any blood bought believer would compromise what God said was right, for what man thought was right. Now I understand that in their minds they thought that it is a form of submission. To every Christian reading this I want to clearly emphasize, that this is not submission to God, but compromising for man. Anytime that we are presented with anything that is contrary to the Word of God, it is our duty to stand for God and respectfully disagree. That' s where I think most of us get lost. We don't know how to disagree with something yet still be submitted. There has been many times that people who have had authority over me, both spiritual and secular, have done things that I didn't necessarily agree with but like David, I didn't come against them or speak to anyone else concerning the situation. I simply told God all about it and watched Him work out the situation. What keeps us out of trouble, as the ones submitting, is our ability, like David, to not agree with something that we see going on, yet still submit to, love, respect, and not talk about the people in leadership. Nowhere in the scripture do you see David talking about Saul to anyone except God. When we can learn to take our problems to God and otherwise be silent, a lot of the problems in our churches would go away. David has modeled a great example before us of how to not agree with something, yet still live a life not restricted by the graveclothe of rebellion.

Anytime that we act in rebellion against those over us we are sinning. James 4:17 lets us know that if we know what to do and don't do it, it is sin. You may say I still have a relationship with God, and in a sense you do, but always remember sin separates you from God. How many relationships have you had in your life when the person you were with wasn't making you happy but you stayed with them for a season? Our rebellion says God I don't think you can handle this. You missed it when you chose Mr./Mrs._____. You might say this isn't true, but all through the Bible we find scenarios where God says prove your heart by your actions.

SLEEPING THROUGH RESURRECTION

> *" But you, lazybones, how long will you sleep? When will you wake up? I want you to learn this lesson: A little extra sleep, a little more slumber, a little folding of the hands to rest- and poverty will pounce on you like a bandit; scarcity will attack you like an armed robber."* — **Proverbs 6: 9-11 NLT**

Laziness is a sickness that truly taken over the body of Christ. To be asleep in this chapter means to be spiritually dormant, stagnate, or sluggish. In an examination of both myself and other saints, I have found that most of us have a problem being committed or showing endurance in anything that we do for God and other wise. It seems that most times we don't have the tenacity or the integrity to finish what we start come what may. Why? I believe that this is a diabolical plot of the devil to cause the body to lackadaisically give up hope in faith in Christ. I can't begin to count the times that I have said during the writing of this book that I would start a new chapter tomorrow; and then one day turns into two, and two into three, and three into three weeks. I chose to examine this particular gravecloth because as I just stated I'm fighting my way free from it right now. It's harder and more harmful then you think.

There are a lot of us who have stood up in the Spirit and in the flesh and said God I will do it, God I will say it, but fail to walk it out. We are living in a generation of believers who get to receive such a wonderful out pouring of God's Spirit and anointing on all people (Joel 2:28), but I often think that this out pouring is taken for granted. We who are called by His Name and given such an anointing often times forget that we must cooperate with the Holy Spirit in order to birth the things that God want us to do in the earth. There are many things that I know that God has called me to do and say in the right season, but even I struggle with the motivation to walk into my destiny in faith when God allows me to see that the appointed vision won't happen for three years. As believers we get lazy, not weary, in our waiting and processing season. We take on the attitude of, "well Father if you said it's not the season for me to preach, I guess I can just relax and be a regular Christian." What we don't realize is that what we do in our winter season is what births the destiny in our due season. The time that I spend now dedicating myself to the service in God's house, to prayer, to fasting, and to the Word is the exact thing that activates the power and anointing to walk into all that God has called me to.

We have to begin to realize that the spirit of laziness will keep us in the tomb. I wonder if before Lazarus died he knew that his sickness was not unto death. Had God already spoken to him before hand and said, "Prepare yourself for the miracle?" Could it be possible that unlike Mary and Martha, when Lazarus felt sickness come upon him, he knew that Jesus would come? If Lazarus did know, what type of preparation went into him approaching death? These are questions that most believers never think about. The Bible doesn't discuss what Lazarus thought or said, but just think about how you would have prepared if God spoke to you in the midnight hour and said that tomorrow your life would be used for His glory. Most of us would put on our Sunday best and go on a 24 hour fast and speak in tongues for three days straight. So, why not do it today? The last thing that Jesus says to His disciples in Luke 16 is that signs shall follow us that believe. I believe that in our waiting periods we forget that ever day is another opportunity for God to use us in any way that He chooses. It may be to do something as simple as smile at someone or as extreme as raise the dead. The point is, we can't hear His call if we choose to stay asleep.

I can only imagine the thoughts that went through Lazarus's head during his sickness and death. "I know that this will not end in death, though the devil says that it is over for me," says Lazarus, "God promised that Jesus is going to use this for His glory so I got be ready. He told me that I might have to leave this body for a minute but He told me to stay alert in the Spirit so that when Jesus calls my name in a couple of days, I'm ready to come back." Can't you just imagine the excitement and faith that Lazarus must have had in this God that we serve, to avail himself enough to be used by God even unto death. Unlike the other graveclothes that we may encounter, laziness is the most subtle. This is basically one of those spirits that the devil doesn't have to monitor or seduce us with much. He already knows that with one introduction, like crack, most believers are hooked. He acts much like a drug dealer in the sense that he knows that the spirit of laziness becomes our drug of choice. He doesn't have to push it on us, we come looking for it. We as a body of believers must step our game up if we are going to win the lost in these last days. We have to begin to unwrap ourselves from the comforts of our flesh. Everything is not always going to be the way that we want it, or go the way we want it, but we have a responsibility to God. We have been purchased with a price, so no matter if we feel like it or not, we have to give God our best in our winter seasons and our due seasons. A lot of us want to just get by on God's grace and mercy. Of course all of us would be consumed without it, but I would like to be one of the men of God who not only was shown God's grace and mercy for what I wasn't able to accomplish in my flesh, but His favor for what I was willing to do and sacrifice for in my flesh. See brothers and sisters its all about the crucifixion of our flesh. Romans 12:1-2 tells us that we are to give God our bodies because it is our reasonable service or the least we can do. I know that as I stated before I have been guilty of being wrapped up by the gravecloth of laziness, but after all that God has done for me in my life, I have a responsibility to always give Him my best. My best includes my time, my prayer life, my Word life, my dedication to the House of God, and even to the preparation of my destiny. Honestly as this world system gets more and more corrupt, a Christian has no business being lazy. We have to get over ourselves in order to reach the masses. Remember it's not about what we feel like doing, it's about us being on post to do what God has called us to do at anytime. I know that sometimes it's hard to get up out of our comfy beds or our comfy situations in order to be effective for God but there is a world that's dying and a God who has called you by name to come forth to do something, through Christ Jesus, to change it.

COMPARATIVE JEALOUSY

"But they are only comparing themselves with each other, and measuring themselves by themselves. What foolishness!"
— **2 Corinthians 10: 12 NLT**

In our lives through the media, school, jobs, and, unfortunately, sometimes in the church, we are taught to compare and compete for value and worth. In order to be important you have to be better than the next man/woman. We are taught that we can gauge our value and being in life based on how much better or worse we are than those surrounding us. I believe that this is where most people have failed to develop an intimate and continual relationship with God. They have allowed the world's mentality to bleed over into the kingdom system. Many believers and non believers now determine their relationship with God based those around them. They say things like, "I must be ok because even though I don't tithe, at least I'm not out there doing drugs." Or either we go to the other extreme by saying, "well everybody got something and I'm not going to stop doing what I'm doing because I've seen some of these Christian folks doing the same things, and even worse." Even though in some cases these examples prove to be true, these proverbial people were never designed to be the standard. When God sent His Son Jesus Christ to earth He, and He alone, became the standard for us to live up to. My walk and dedication to God has nothing to do with what others around me are doing or saying. I have a reason and responsibility to actively pursue the God who pursued me. It was the Apostle Peter who spoke up in John 6:53-69 when Jesus told His followers that in order to be His followers they would have to eat of His flesh and drink of His blood to be His disciples, and many of them left Him and followed Him no more, and then Jesus turned to the twelve disciples and asked them would they also leave Him. It was Peter who said those powerful words that every believer should echo in their spirit and audibly every day; "To whom shall we go? For it is only you who have the words of eternal life." As believers we share the obligation to follow Christ no matter what those around us decide to do. When we slow up or stop due to or relation to those around us we allow our relationship with people to out weigh our relationship with God. When we allow our comparisons with other people to determine our standing with God our actions are telling God forget the example of your Christ, Bob's example is the one I choose to live up to.

The worst thing that a parent can do is compare their children. Most parents don't realize the danger in trying to fit every one of their children into one mold. So many parents beat down their children's self esteem and creativity by trying to make the infinite expressive God fit His unique expressions into the same box. God created all of us to add something unique to the earth to do something in a unique way as only you can. When we cause our children to feel bad about their creative yet righteous differences, it welcomes anther gravecloth, rejection, to bind them. Causing a person to feel bad about who God, emphasis on God, is calling them to be causes them nothing more than confusion, which we know that God is not the author of. Most parents that are reading this book are probably saying that's not me, I would never do that to my child, but anytime that you start a sentence off with your with why can't you be more like_____ or _____ would never do/say something like that, your doing it. As parents we must ask the Holy Spirit to give us a strategy to encourage and guide or kids in a way that allows them to still be unique expressions of God. Comparisons among children have so many adverse effects. It breeds insecurity, resentment, jealousy, etc. I believe this what happened in Genesis 4:1-10 with Cane and Able. Cane's sacrifice was unacceptable to God but Abel's was. I believe that through this occurrence Satan used the gravecloth of comparison to drive Cain to kill his brother. I'm sure some of the thoughts of the devil that Cain allowed himself to dwell on were, why was mine not acceptable but Abel's was?, What has Able don that's better than me?, He probably thinks he's better than me, and if I kill him then I would become God's favorite. Able became despised in his brother's eyes all because his brother's failures caused him to compare himself to a standard that really wasn't a standard at all.

For many years of my life I felt ugly, unattractive, and unlovable because I compared myself to the movies, the music videos, and the other guys around me that girls were going for. Since that time my self image has improved and I have lost a substantial amount of weight, but it has taken me years to unwrap from that gravecloth. The people that I compared myself to made me feel like I would never meet a woman to love me because I would never be able to match up with them. I believe that many men and women go through this believing that because they are not the thinnest, or most athletic, or lightest that they will never be able to find themselves beautiful. These two words are for you, Stop Comparing!!!! I do believe that we need to be healthy and there are extra problems that come with being over weight, but do not fret over things about yourself that you can't naturally change. Weight is something that can be naturally altered through exercise and proper eating but God created you with certain qualities that need not be augmented. Surgically altering things means God made a mistake on you, when He never makes mistakes. There are many people who believe that men don't suffer with low self esteem, but that is a lie. We go through, we hurt, and cry in the dark, but we are taught not to express it. Women you must begin to build men up because just like you we have insecurities that need healing. To my brothers I encourage you to devour the Word like never before so that you can see how much God loves you and how beautiful He says you are. That's the only thing that will transform your mind. As believers we have to begin to believe the Word of God as reality. We walk by faith and not by sight. It doesn't matter what the world says about us because one day it will pass away, but what God says about you is what will be forever written in the heavens and eternity. Brothers remember it was David, a man, that encouraged himself by saying, "I am fearfully and wonderfully made." One thing that most non-vain brothers don't do is look at and analyze themselves in the mirror. Brothers I encourage you everyday to get up and spend five minutes in the mirror looking at yourself and encouraging yourself in the Word and telling yourself that you're fearfully and wonderfully made until you feel it in your spirit and are transformed by the Word. I do want to let you know that even with weight, the messed up hair, the acne, etc., you must know that you are fearfully and wonderfully made, so that when that outward change takes place, it is just and outward expression of an inward knowing.

The gravecloth of comparison is something that I have experienced a lot through my experience in the music world. In a society that, even in Christian music, is looking for the next big thing, you are always tempted to compromise creativity for acceptance and fame. If you look at the music industry most times you find that it is no longer about creativity and getting a word from God for an expression in the earth, it's about finding out who is hot and following the trend of riding their coat tails. That's when you find fifty people/groups looking and sounding just like Kirk Franklin, Tye Tribbett, Martha Munizzi, or Third Day. Because of what's comfortable and profitable, no one wants to step out of the boat. I believe that we do a great disservice both to God and the lost because while we should be reaching this person over here, we are too busy trying to be the next somebody else. This causes the person over here to not be able to receive from us because he couldn't receive from the person before you that you are trying to be. We have to make sure that in us doing music for God we are chasing souls and not audiences. Earlier on when I first started writing and singing I would beat myself up because I didn't sound like Fred Hammond, or Donnie McKlurkin, or J Moss. I compared myself and wanted to give up, even though I know I was called, because I kept comparing myself to the standard of their work. Recently God told me that we have been putting chains on Him musically. God is looking to put new music in the earth, but we are so busy trying to be the fake somebody else to sell a record that we can't birth the new sound that would help, through the Word, to set the captive free. That's why it is such a pull on the saints when it comes to secular music because even though there are those artists who are knock offs of someone else, there are more artist that dare to be different. So Bradley are you saying that God is giving these vulgar singers these new sounds? Yes, in a sense. God is trying to get a new thing in the earth and He will use who ever is available. I do believe that most of them receive the new sound and pervert it for a use that glorifies things contrary to God's Word, but they are still available, where many of us are too bound by a traditional/ religious spirit or to profit or fan oriented to receive it. There needs to be more artists that have been called by God who dare to be different. There are a few who blazed there own trail like Lisa Mcclendon, Kim Burrell, The Clark Sisters, Canton Jones, and J.R. but there is a need for more. There are too many souls out there that need Jesus to be stuck comparing and copying someone else. The world can tell a fake from the real. We need to develop an ear to hear God and develop our unique being in order to bless the nations. I look at myself being eclectic inside of the realm of Christiandom. Some artists that I listen to that are divers but continue to bless me, other than the ones previously named, are Christafari (Christian Reggae), Kierra Sheard (Urban Gospel), 21:03 (Urban Gospel), GI (Urban Gospel), Virtue (Urban Gospel), Matt Kearney (Christian Bluegrass), Da Truth (Christian Rap), Sarah Brendel (Christian Pop), and Toby Mac (Christian All Over). These artist stay in their lane and keep an ear to hear from God to relay it in the earth. They are all different with different audiences, but all they continue to bless and win souls to the body.

When it comes to music many religious/tradition bound Christians would say that God doesn't operate on anything new but only in the traditional Mahalia Jackson or James Cleveland way of doing things. To say this would mean that not only is God one dimensional, but His is not the God expressed in His Word. If you recall in the book of Acts and the following Pauline Epistles, the ministry of Paul, at times Barnabas, and Peter were very different. Paul was sent to the Gentiles wile Peter was sent the Jews. Paul's verbiage and style of presenting the oracles of God to the Jews was many times more direct than that of Peter. Barnabas and Paul even split way for a season because of their different ministry points and styles. They all had different way of relaying the Gospel, but all the messages and styles were given by the same spirit. To say that only one musical style to spread the Gospel is effective, is to say that the God of that one musical style is not the same God who sent out Paul, Barnabas, and Peter. Always remember:

> *"The human body has many parts, but the many parts make up only one body. So it is with the body of Christ. Some of us are Jews, some are Gentiles, some are slaves, and some are free. But we all have been baptized into Christ's body by one Spirit, and we have all received the same Spirit. Yes, the body has many different parts, not just one part. If the foot says, " I am not a part of the body because I am not a hand," that does not make it any less a part of the body. An if the ear says, " I am not part of the body because I am only an ear and not an eye," would that make it any less a part of the body? Suppose the whole body were just one big ear, how could you smell anything? But God made our bodies with many parts, and he has put each part just where he wants it. What a strange thing a body would be if it had only one part! Yes, there are*

many parts, but only one body. The eye can never say to the hand, " I don't need you." The head can't say to the feet, "I don't need you." In fact, some of the parts that seem weakest and least important are really the most necessary. And the parts we regard as less honorable are those we clothe with the greatest care. So we carefully protect from the eyes of others those parts that should not be seen, while other parts do not require this special care. So God has put the body together in such a way that extra honor and care are given to those parts that have less dignity. This makes for harmony among the members, so that all the members care for each other equally. — **I Corinthians 12:12-25 NLT**

The Power Of Control

"But there was a certain man, called Simon, which beforetime in the same city used sorcery, and bewitched the people of Samaria, giving out that himself was some great one: To whom they all gave heed, from the least to the greatest, saying, This man is the great power of God. And to him they had regard because that of long time he had bewitched them with sorceries." — **Acts 8: 9-11 KJV**

Controlling people is witchcraft! One of the biggest bondages, or graveclothes, to the body of Christ is the spirit of control. Never in all my life have I seen so many people fighting for dominance in relationships, friendships, and families. It almost seems like most people find their self esteem in how many people they can dominate and bring under their control. It seems to be an epidemic in the body of Christ to have spiritual blood clots. Some may be saying, "What are spiritual blood clots?" Well, physically a blood clot is a coagulation of cells or tissue, or matter that causes a blockage in the body that prevents blood flow. That blockage can cause the human body severe complications and, in severe cases, even death. This same principle translates into the spiritual realm in the form of spiritual blood clots. These clots often times operate as cliques in the church. These cliques become blockages in the body that prevent the life giving Spirit to flow throughout the body of Christ as we win souls. They hinder the power of God from moving in the earth through his people by hindering those in the body by causing the people in the body to operate in fear instead of faith, on opinions rather than on the Word, and in practices instead of power. God wants to use people but cliques causes the people in the body to be so messed up that it limits or hinders what God wants to do in the earth to bless, heal, deliver, and save others. They coagulate the body or stop the flow. Cliques are something that most people don't believe that they're in, even though the art of exclusion is something that they major on.

A clique is something that is designed not only to dominate a person's behavior, but their mind, their time, and their lifestyle. Often times cliques are utilized to break down and reshape a person's whole being into the image of, not God but, the person that is the King/Queen bee of that particular clique. Be careful of those people who you surround yourself with that have a hard time allowing you to be the unique expression of God that you are. Be careful of those who tell you, without a word from the Lord, that you need to change this or that in order to be in their good graces or the perfect will of God. These people are often those who have their own graveclothes from their past choking them so tightly that they have to do something to feel powerful or liberated. Often people who are over cliques have been tormented in their lives by past failures or hurts from what their parents didn't do, what their parents didn't say, from not ever having their opinions heard or expressed, or from never being able to be the leader over anything. So now the devil has used all of the past hurt in their lives to help to pervert their outlook on life into having to dominate over everyone that comes into their lives. The result then becomes that the hurt, hurts other people through the use of control.

In Acts 8 you find the story of Simon. Simon was a sorcerer in the city of Samaria who found away to appeal to what the people needed the most, a savior. The Bible lets us know that Simon had bewitched the people, or used witchcraft to control the minds and thoughts of the people. Most people that dominate control over others have simply found a way to meet a need that the people have not yet discovered can only be met in Christ Jesus. During this time after the ascension of Jesus there must have been a great confusion among the Jews about the identity of this man named

Jesus. The confusion of was he or wasn't he the Messiah must have swept through every town including the city of the "half breeds," Samaria. Imagine the confusion that their must have been for the Samaritans. Not only were they ostracized by the Jews, but they must have been confused about their identity with God. They must have believed that the Messiah would come, but they didn't have the same experiences with him that the other Jewish people of the time had. Jesus did have an encounter with the woman at the well, but they didn't have the same opportunities to sit at the feet of the Savior and learn of Him like the people of Jerusalem or Galilee did. They were not welcome among the Jews because they were seen as not a part of the Jewish nation because they were a mix of both Jewish and Gentile blood; in this time that would be the same as a Pagan and a Christian having a child together. Imagine the confusion of the people of Samaria remembering a vague encounter with this man named Jesus but never really having assurance that this same man has come to reconcile them to the father. They had a need to have the hurt of rejection and low self esteem and of confusion healed by a God that was greater than them.

Then this man, from out of town, named Simon comes along. This man doesn't radiate of the same love that Jesus did, neither does he possess the same wisdom or compassion that He had, yet he does do many miracles that the people of Samaria had never seen done before. It seems that when people lack hope or assurance in something, when anything that comes along that has the slightest aroma of being something better or provides hope, they will give themselves to it. Most hurt people just don't want to feel the pain anymore. Not to be healed, just not to feel the pain anymore. Simon came along and did these great miracles among them and Bible says that he bewitched the people and they began to look upon him as a great one. Most people, who turn to drugs, alcoholism, sexual sin, etc., become bewitched or entrapped by that thing because it provides a temporary solution for an internal problem. Most people who have ever been addicted to crack cocaine will tell you, "I did it because I just wanted to feel better and before I knew it it had a hold on me." The spirit of bewitchment or control has a way of sneaking up on the unsuspecting. You think for a while that you are just giving in to this person or these people here and there, or submitting your will and your opinions to them, and not God, here and there, until you find out that you are involved in a relationship that has put you under a bondage that will take the power of God to get you from under.

Most people involved in the church of Jim Jones found themselves in the same situation. These people thought they had found someone who gave them something that they had never felt before, love and acceptance. Many of the people in Jim Jones' church had been rejected by the world because of the times. Many were racial oppressed, socially oppressed, estranged from their families, living homosexual and lesbian life styles, and just down trodden by life. Jones seemed to provide a safe haven for them from the outside world where they would not be judged and were free to be them. I must interject this point, in 2 Peter 2:19 the Bible lets us know that often times the people who bewitch people with control by promising freedom and liberty, are often the ones bound by something that they cannot control. The people who tried to find soles in Jones found that his teaching had bewitched them into giving up their lives. Those who did escape before hand began to realize that the same thing that they thought would heal their hurt, was the same thing that was actually helping to cause it to grow.

The Bible leads me to believe that the graveclothes of control that Simon was using could have been a clue to his past. In later verses the Bible says that when Phillip went down to Samaria and preached the things concerning the Lord Jesus Christ and the Kingdom of God that the people believed and were baptized. Then it goes on to say that even Simon, after seeing the signs following the Word of God that Phillip preached, believed and was baptized. This leads me to believe that the bewitchment that

Simon had worked on the people was only a reproduction of the bewitchment that was going on in his own life. Most people who control other people have either been controlled or never been in control of their own lives and are now acting out since the opportunity presents itself. Simon probably bewitched the people because he felt powerless in his life. Acts 8 tells us that Simon was astonished by the signs and wonders that Phillip had done among them. Simon longed to find a resting place in a true in living God where not only was there healing, but where there was true power. Simon didn't get saved to harness the power of God, but I believe that he gave his life to the Lord because he found that the power or control that he thought he had meant nothing and that the only true purpose or importance rests in faith in Christ Jesus.

I want to leave you in this chapter with a few ways to determine if you have been sucked into a clique and are placing or being placed under another person's control. Wherever you find your self in the following list just know that there is deliverance and healing in Christ Jesus you don't have to stay bound in controlling or being controlled once you locate yourself through the Word of God and prayer.

You are causing spiritual blood clots in the body of Christ through cliques if:

1. You can only hang with certain people.
2. You get upset if your friends want to hang with someone else or include someone else in the group.
3. If you tell or are told through words, actions, or looks to keep certain people out of the group.
4. Like Simon, you have to be the leader or center of your group at all times.

5. You constantly are involved in conversations putting down other people that are not in your group.

6. Your circle of people shrinks solely based on the emotions or mood of the leader.

7. You are not allowed to interact with people, even those in your own family.

8. You have to have a reason or explanation for doing or not doing something for people outside and in the group.

9. Your pastor no longer is the leader of you church but the leader of the group is.

10. Your pastor's counsel, through the Word of God, in your life becomes less and less important and the counsel of the leader of the clique becomes more and more dominant.

11. You change your opinion or words based on the mood or reaction of the people in your group.

12. The people in your group get mad when you don't take their opinions or advice.

13. You compromise the Word of God to still be a part of the group.

14. Life decisions are made not through fasting, prayer, the Word of God, and Godly counsel, but based on what the leader of the clique dictates.

15. You have to give a detailed report of what you said to the pastor to the clique, if you sought the pastor's counsel.

I do want to say one thing. There isn't anything wrong with having friends that you primarily hang with do to similar interest, hobbies, and history. What makes you come under bondage is when any one person in the group has always got to be dominant over the others and you are no longer able to be an individual. Check your relationships to make sure that this isn't you or someone else in your group. I didn't share this with you for you to just totally abandon those in the clique, but to throw you a life line which is the Word of God so that both you and they can come out of it. Galatians 6:1 tells us that those of us who are spiritual have the responsibility to restore. If the clique's members are willing to come out of what they are in once, in love, you share this message with them, think about how deeper your friendship will grow and how you are helping the body of Christ to progress forward. Remember the bewitcher Simon was saved through the power and presentation of the Word of God. Don't count anyone out if you haven't presented it to them.

THE LURE OF LUST

"David's son Absalom had a beautiful sister named Tamar.
And Amnon, her half brother, fell desperately in love with her.
Amonon became so obsessed with Tamar that he became ill.
She was a virgin, and it seemed impossible that he could ever
fulfill his love for her. Now Amnon had a very crafty friend- his
cousin Jonadab. He was the son of David's brother Shimea. One
day Jonadab said to Amnon, "What's the trouble? Why should
the son of a king look so dejected morning after morning?" So
Amnon told him, "I am in love with Tamar, Absalom's sister."
"Well," Jonadab said, "I'll tell you what to do. Go back to bed
and pretend you are sick. When your father comes to see you, ask
him to let Tamar come and prepare some food for you. Tell him
you'll feel better if she feeds you." So Amnon pretended to be
sick. And when the king came to see him, Amnon asked him,
"Please let Tamar come to take care of me and cook something
for me to eat." So David agreed and sent Tamar to Amnon's
house to prepare some food for him. When Tamar arrived at
Amnon's house, she went to the room where he was lying down
so he could watch her mix some dough. Then she backed some
special bread for him. But when she set the serving tray before
him, he refused to eat. "Everyone get out of here," Amnon told
his servants. So they all left. The he said to Tamar, "Now bring
the food into my bedroom and feed it to me here." So Tamar
took it to him. But as she was feeding him, he grabbed her and
demanded, "Come to be with me, my darling sister." "No, my
brother!" she cried. "Don't be foolish! Don't do this to me! You
what a serious crime it is to do such a thing in Israel. Where
could I go in my shame? And you would be called on of the
greatest fools in Israel. Please, just speak to the king about it,
and he will let you marry me." But Amnon wouldn't listen to
her, and since he was stronger than she was, he raped her. Then
suddenly Amnon's love turned to hate, and he hated her even
more than he had loved her." — **2 Sam. 13:1-15 (NLT)**

Lust seems to be one of the most noticeable spirits running ramped both outside and inside of the church. I know with the beginning of this chapter some of my religious readers might be saying, "Now why is he telling everybody that lust is ramped in the church, that's going to make non believers not want to be a part." My response to that is simply this, God doesn't operate in appearances; He operates in the spirit of Truth. The key to deliverance is not acting like everything is okay on the outside, but getting to the root of the problem so that you are actually are okay on the inside. Church people, not the body of Christ, for too long have wanted to perpetrate the façade that everybody in it is perfect when that isn't the condition. Church people use that appearance to let everybody else know that they believe they have arrived, while the true body of Christ simply says that everyday and in every way I'm believing God that the things that I used to do and be, Jesus has given me a way to be free from them. We're living in a time when you see the traces of problems and graveclothes on people that have not yet been stripped from their lives and ultimately from the church. This is the era where you hear about people in and out of the church doing crazy, perverse, and sexual things with the opposite sex, the same sex, children, animals, and even inanimate objects. It seems that the graveclothe of lust has bound the majority of the world in some area of their lives. It seems that whether it be sexual, monetary, possessions, or power, most people have something that their lusting for or something that they will do anything to get.

Within the Body of Christ this should not be. The only thing that we as the people of the living God should be violently pursuing is God. We have to be careful that the people or the things that we have don't become the God that we pursue. A lot of us would say that that's not the situation that we find ourselves in, but how much time do you spend talking on the phone compared to the time that you spend talking to God? How much effort do you expend to get to work or to see you girlfriend/boyfriend compared to the amount of effort you expend trying to get to church? How much mental energy do you utilize like Amnon to get that woman/man out of their draws compared to the energy you utilize to meditate on the Word and things of God? Don't tell me that there's not one thing that you don't lust after. Once again this book is not designed to bash you, but to uncover where the devil is operating in your life so that through the exercising of your faith, coupled with the Word, you can serve him an eviction notice.

When I think of my own life and the times that I've found myself caught up in a lustful situation it amazes me. There have been periods in my life where I've allowed the graveclothe of lust to engulf my whole body with the opposite sex. I have been in situations with young ladies that I should not have been in do to crafty planning on my part. Parents one thing that I will advise you to do is to never underestimate the craftiness of your kids. I do realize that no parent can watch their children twenty four hours a day, but make sure that your kids are in a safe environment when a way from you. What I mean by this is that I have been in places and done things in my life before I got saved that my parents had no idea of. I have been over at young ladies houses unsupervised by either my or their parents for extended periods of time. I have been at others friend's houses with young ladies for extended periods of time when my parents thought there was parental supervision. Whether you realize it or not parents, all parents are not saved and honest. There are other people's parents who will lie for your child and set up situations for your child to go down the wrong path. I'm not trying to make any parent be over protective of their child but to ask them to simply be discerning of the friends and words that your child tells you. All kids are going to do things that they have no business, but I believe that the job of a parent is to do your very best to make sure that the bad choices that they make doesn't hinder them for the rest, or a great portion, of their lives. There are things that I have had to fight out of since I got saved, that I wouldn't have had to if I would have simply listened to my mom. Make no mistake about it parents, teenagers in the church are having sex and doing things that even a person like myself who's only a couple of years older has never thought of. We have to expose the devil's operation in their lives so they can begin to be delivered for destiny. One thing I know is that lust spirits don't leave just because you, or your child, finally decides that they're/you're ready to get serious about God. As a matter of fact it's at that time that the graveclothe of lust wants to become the most active in the soul and flesh of you and your child. There are many amazing men and women of God that fought for years before they finally were unwrapped from the graveclothe of lust. Why allow you or your child to go down that path when it can be avoided by monitoring the things that you or your family put before you and around you?

Like most people Amnon's sin began in his mind. Amnon allowed the devil to speak to his mind until he got to a place where he was convinced that he was in love with his sister. The Bible said that he became so convinced that he made himself sick. What the devil always does to people is start off by giving them thoughts. These thoughts are his first line of attack to penetrate your armor (Ephesians 6). The devil sends thoughts to the mind of the believer about people and situations regarding lust. These thoughts may be an instant replay of things that the believer has done or seen in the past or something new that the devil concocted especially for them. If the devil sees that the believer has received these thoughts or is meditating on these thoughts, then he intensifies them to further bind the mind of the believer. Amnon in the beginning of 2 Sam. 13 found himself in this exact situation. I'm sure that the devil started his obsession off with Tamar slowly. He probably had seen his sister and thought about or spoke about how beautiful she was. From that the devil saw his opportunity to invade. The Word of God lets us know that we are to cast down every imagination and every high thing that exalteth itself against the knowledge of God, according to 2 Cor.10:5, but when this is not done continually the devil begins to invade the soulish realm and fill it with thoughts to convince the mind. Many of the people that you see walking around in lesbian, homosexual, abusive, and ungodly relationships have had their minds convinced that there is nothing wrong with the relationship. It's almost like in the movies when a person is captured by the enemy and they get brain washed by the enemy to the extent that they believe that the people that were once their allies, are now their foes. I Timothy 4:2 speak of the devil searing the conscience of people as with a hot iron. This is what the enemy can do with the grave clothe of lust.

Amnon entertained the thoughts for too long. What the devil often does after having the person meditate on the thoughts for so long till they are convinced in their minds, is that he then allows the person to feel it or believe in their hearts and flesh. This is what happened to Amnon. The Bible says that he became so obsessed with his sister that he became ill. The thoughts and perversion of the devil displayed themselves in Amnon's body through a physical sickness. Most young men who are in a saved relationship that has received the devil's thoughts will begin to have sexual symptoms in their body. I have talked with friends who have said that they have felt physical pain in their genital area from not having sex, even if they have not had sex in several years. In most cases, what has happened is the devil has been talking to the young man's mind so long that they now feel like there is a physical need to have it. Most times they begin to be led more by their flesh then their spirit at this point which is exactly what the devil wants. After the devil gave Amnon physical symptoms in his body he sent him someone to help in the process of sin. Be careful of those people who come into your life in the weakest points of your walk. Those who come under the appearance of caring, but have actually tapped into the demonic plans of the devil and come to help to see it through. These people, like Jonadab, will often reaffirm the thoughts that the devil has given you and help you in the process of falling from grace. It was Amnon's cousin Jonadab who came along and gave him the strategy to succeed in raping his sister Tamar. It was Jonadab who demonically sensed his cousin's problem and knew exactly how to speak to his emotions to get it to be carried out in his flesh. The devil knows how to send people into your life at just the right season to cater to your emotions and to cater to your flesh in attempt to get you out of the will of God. Often these people will come into your life at just the right time with a strategy that totally contradicts the Word yet pleases your flesh. In this way the devil tried to mimic God. Often times when we can't clearly hear what God is saying or need confirmation of what we believe God is saying, He will send us a believer who acts as a prophet/ prophetess to give us a Word that keeps us on the right path. The Jonadabs come into our lives to help to prophesy the demonic destiny of the believer. Most people fall into this trap because the things that the Jonadab tells us line up with what we have been thinking or feeling. One thing you should always remember is that the devil can tell when you have received his thoughts because your eventually will act them out in your flesh and speak it out of your mouth; for example, you use to not watch porno's now your watching them, you use to not entertain staying all night at your girl's house but now you start staying over there later and later, and you used to not look at things that had same sex people kissing and being together now suddenly you become interested in it. The devil sees by these actions that his thoughts are working on you, so then comes Jonadab to give you a strategy and confirmation of how to walk out of the will of God.

The graveclothe of lust is something that many believers suffer with in silence. Many are too afraid to talk about it among the other saints because of a fear that they will not seem spiritual or holy. This is foolishness. There is supposed to be a continual operation in the church of the healing and delivering power of Jesus. We should be able to talk about the issues that we face as believers so that we all can help one another to find a solution in the Word of God. Before I gave my life to the Lord in 2004 I really struggled with the graveclothe of lust manifested in the spirit masturbation and pornography. I didn't get free from it until I attended a college men's retreat and heard the pastor of the church speak about his struggle in the past with the same issue and how Jesus had delivered him from it. At that moment my faith went to another level and I was set free by the power of God because of his testimony (Revelations 12:11). We can't get rid of the devil's trappings, or graveclothes, if we are afraid to expose where they lay in our lives. The devil operates in silence and half truths. Expose to God the areas of your life that are not yet free and the truth of where the root lies so that he can destroy the root and break the yoke that the devil thought he had on you by His spirit.

THE PRIDEFUL ENEMY

"So Absalom went to Hebron. But while he was there, he sent secret messengers to every part of Israel to stir up a rebellion against the king. "As soon as you hear trumpets," his message read, "you will know that Absalom has been crowned king in Hebron." He took two hundred men from Jerusalem with him as guests, but they knew nothing of his intentions. While he offering the sacrifices, he sent for Ahithophel, one of David's counselors who lived in Giloh. Soon many others joined Absalom, and the conspiracy gained momentum. A messenger soon arrived in Jerusalem to tell King David, "All Israel has joined Absalom in a conspiracy against you!" — **2 Sam. 15: 9-13**

Pride is one of the main elements that limits the life changing power of God. In the *New Strong's Exhaustive Concordance of the Bible* pride is defined as a conceited sense of one's superiority. This graveclothe makes it hard for the transforming power of God to penetrate the believer's heart mainly because it is an act of the believers will. Although all acts, in one way or another, are act of a person's will, pride has a special influence do to the fact that it can be turned on or off at the will of the person.

Many people that are blinded by pride don't even realize the possession or bondage that it has become in their life. Often times pride gives the afflicted person a false sense of reality which blinds them from correctly viewing the truth. Pride has often entrapped many famous pastors of yesteryear to the point that they lost their ministries because they failed to realize the actions they were taking were no longer anointed, appointed, or endorsed by God. Many mainstream ministries that were mightily used of

God at one time fizzled out because the leadership became more consumed with selfish motivations and the praise of the people than the anointing and the will of God.

Pride, more than anything else that I have ever seen, has the capability of hardening the heart to change. Often times we can find so many people who were once vibrant loving people that have allowed pride through situations to disqualify them from destiny. How many of us have known a woman that could have been our wives but disqualified themselves from us and their over all destiny because they were unwilling to change in an area were God was demanding a transformation? Or how many women have ever known a man who could have been the next Bill Gates but because his pride excelled faster than his creative ideas, he never made it to the top of the corporate ladder? The Bible is telling the truth in Prov. 16:18 when it says that pride comes before a fall. Pride is one thing that can most definitely hinder a person's ability to successfully hear and carry out the will of God for their life. It is almost like a person that voluntarily places themselves in a 12 foot thick cave and can no longer hear what's going in the world on the outside of that cave. They may feel that they're safe but they will never be able to hear the instructions of how to come out of it.

Absalom's pride began as soon as his sister was raped by their brother. Absalom was furious at the fact that his sister was raped and the Bible lets us know that from the moment that Absalom heard of the rape of his sister Tamar, he hated his brother Amnon. From that very moment Absalom allowed the devil to come into his mind and have place in a plot to kill his brother Amnon. Absalom's plot took two years to come to fruition but it did, resulting in the murder of his brother. I'm sure that one of the contributing factors of why Absalom allowed pride to take root in his heart against his father was due to the way that King David handled, or didn't handle, the rape of Tamar. The Bible never states that David implemented any type of punishment for what Amnon had done to his sister. Like most children that feel that there parents have not handled a situation properly, Absalom probably believed that he needed to take matters into his own hands to defend his sister's honor. After Amnon's murder Absalom fled from the kingdom and stayed with his grandfather for three years hoping that his father's anger would have subsided by then. Then Absalom, through a trick, was allowed back into his father's palace but was not allowed in his father's presence. This was another factor that helped to bind Absalom in pride. Can you imagine having your parent allow you to live with them after you have made a major mistake but saying they don't want to see you? Imagine the thoughts of bitterness and resentment that would be flowing through your mind even though you were the initial person in the wrong. Always remember that bitterness and resentment are often the companions of pride. Most of the times they serve as the main arteries to pump pride into your heart. Absalom probably felt as though his father was being unfair and that his brother should have been the one to flee from the kingdom after what he had done to Tamar not Absalom. Think about the time Absalom must have spent alone in his section of the palace meditating on all the mistakes that he had seen his father make over Israel, and all of the things he must have thought he would handle better if he were the king over Israel.

Most people that become hardened by pride don't get that way over night. Becoming prideful is a process. Absalom had to have rehearsed in his mind for months all the things that his father King David wasn't, before he decided to plot a rebellion against him. Most people who try snatch or rebel against authority have allowed the devil to talk to their minds for months or even years before they act out the imaginations in their body. Like others, I'm sure that the devil had fed Absalom lies of how great he was and how he would be a better king than David, and how he was absolutely right to kill Amnon, and how David should have seen that if he was truly anointed to be king by God. Like Absalom, many people fail to realize that regardless of a leaders mistake it up to God, and him alone, to remove people from power. God does things decently and in order, so he will never call you to come against leadership in rebellion. If you are saying wait a minute, what if my leader is doing _____ I should let it go on unopposed? I'm still saying trust God. It's God's job to raise up and remove people; He doesn't need your help! To act in any other way is rooted in pride in either your confidence to be a better leader, or in your ability to handle a situation better than God.

Proverbs 16:18 lets us see that wherever in our lives pride is operating failure will follow. It is quite possible to be humble in one area of our lives but prideful in another; for example, I can have no problem with submitting to my pastor, but have a problem with thinking I'm the finest dude in my church. That could result in me being successful in submitting in my church but being unsuccessful in a marriage. I have succeeded in one area of my life but because of pride, I have failed in another. There are many marriages in the church failing for this very reason. Spouses have areas in their lives where the Word of God and their spouse is telling them is a problem, yet because they feel that they are alright, they are unwilling to change. A husband might tell his wife for years that she is not supportive when it comes to his ideas, yet his wife won't do anything to improve upon that area. Year after year goes by until the deep commitment that they once had no longer exist and they are more like roommates that husband and wife. The husband's heart is breaking because one of the areas that he needs his wife the most, is the very area that his wife won't help him in. The other side of the spectrum is where you'll find a wife who is not being satisfied intimately by her husband but when she tells him about it he goes off and tells her the problem has to be her. Instead of trusting his wife enough to be his best friend and teach him the things that he might not know about her body, he allows Satan to puff up his ego to the point that his mind becomes hardened to the very idea that he might possibly need to change. Now both he and his wife grow to despise one another because neither one of their needs are being met in the relationship. Be careful of the areas and ideas, not specifically expressed in the Word of God, that you say are off limits to change because those can be the very areas that cause you to step outside of the perfect will of God, or miss out on God's very best for your life.

LOVE MOTIVATES THE MIRACLE

"When Jesus saw her weeping and saw the other people wailing with her, he was moved with indignation and was deeply troubled. "Where have you put him?" he asked them. They told him, "Lord, come and see." Then Jesus wept. "The people who were standing nearby said, "See ho much he loved him."" — **John 11: 33-36 (NLT)**

It is the love of Jesus who will make all the difference as you transform and help others to be unwrapped. Love changes everything since we know according to I John 4:8 that God is love. As we go out to minister healing and deliverance to those that we know are still struggling in their salvation; we must do it in the spirit of love that God has expressed toward us. It is only when our actions are motivated by pure love that God can truly get the glory out of the things that we do for Him. Our motivation can't be for acclaim, pride, selfishness, or status, but for the love of the people of God and our desire to see them set free.

The lesson of love is something that I'm not ashamed to say that I am still learning. I really love the people of God and want to see everyone saved, delivered, healed, and restored, but I am still striving to see and love people the way that Christ did. Christ loved people with a perfect love that looked beyond every fault, action, mess up, and rebellion. That is something that I'm still trying to master. As believers we have to develop a level of love for people that looks past their present day actions and characteristics, and seeks to uncover

the root cause of their actions and see them unwrapped from
it. It would be easy to see someone that drinks and assume
that they drink because they like the taste of alcohol; but it
takes real love to see a person that drinks and want to uncover
the fact that the reason they drink may be something as
devastating as they were sexually molested as a child, and still
want to help them be delivered from that root. We must love
people enough to dig deep and give them the Word of God
not just in conversation, but in action in order to see them
set free. Nobody does anything just because they do it. There
is always a root cause to the actions that are manifesting
themselves in a person.

It was Jesus love and compassion for the people that
motivated the miracle of Jesus raising Lazarus from the dead.
The Bible says that Jesus looked upon the people as they wept
and felt compassion for them. The Lord Jesus felt the pain of
the people. Jesus loved them so much that he didn't want to see
them cry or mourn, so that motivated him to do something
for them. Even though Jesus already knew that it was the will
of the Father to raise Lazarus from the dead, he still displayed
intense love and compassion for the people before raising
Lazarus from the dead. Not only did Jesus display a love for
the people but a love for Lazarus by weeping before the people
at the tomb. Lazarus, Mary, and Martha were friends of Jesus,
and even though he knew the final destination of Lazarus, he
still missed the friendship of the momentarily deceased man.
That's the type of compassion and love we must have for the
lost. The Bible describes them as being spiritually dead. We as
believers must begin to develop a stronger hunger to become
an active part in seeing the lost saved and delivered. There are
dozens of people in our families that we say that we love and
cherish, yet it is no big deal to us that they are not saved. I'm
not suggesting quoting scriptures to them every five minutes,
but we should love them enough to labor for them in prayer,
fasting, and in living a Godly life in front of them. Our love

should be expressed in our actions. Jesus loved Lazarus, so it motivated Him to do something about His dead friend. What it your love for people motivating you to do?

There are people in my life who are not saved or bound by something that keeps them from truly walking out their destiny in Christ Jesus. I want to see them set free, but I have to love them enough to do things to draw them. It may take me allowing them to call me at 3 A.M. to talk, or to ride with them to the store with cursing music blaring, it may take me talking to them while their drunk or high, or most commonly living a Godly life around them continually so they see that the transforming power of God is real. We must love people enough to do something if we want to see people saved and free. There are many people in my life that I'm believing God, in this year, will be saved, delivered, and healed. It's going to take work on my part but I love them enough to do it. A major portion of my part is to still believe the report of the Lord despite what I see them doing. We must remember that sometimes our goal is greater than our struggle. There will be times when we are uncomfortable in life, but we must remember that in the midst of all that's going on in this world, our main goal is to restore people to the kingdom of God. Love produces that passion and tenacity in us to want to see people saved and unwrapped. One thing we must always remember is that God loved us so much that He looked past everything that we thought, did, and said and still drew us to Himself. He could have chosen anybody, but He wanted to use some messed up people like us. In our eyes there are so many people better equipped to do the work of the Lord, yet He still chose to use you and me. That's a love motivated miracle.

Remember, no matter where you are in your walk with Christ Jesus, He loves you enough to want to see you come out whatever is hindering you. He died for you and rose for you, and He wants to see you capitalizing on all the benefits of His resurrection. He lives so you can be totally delivered from whatever the devil thinks that he has on you. As a blood bought believer you have a right to be free from what he says you are. Put your faith in the work of what Christ has done and in the name of Jesus I decree that you will be unwrapped!!!

EPILOGUE

I hope in this journey God has revealed to you the area where He wants to see you free in. My prayer is and will always be that the people of God realize that just because you have been a certain way or in a certain way all your life, doesn't mean that you have to always bee that way. Whether its drugs, alcohol, promiscuity, etc. God has made a way for your escape. God wants to see all of His children enjoying the abundant life here on earth, not just when we get to heave. It is never too late for you to change.

There has never been such a time in American history where it has been so hard to get rid of bad habits. It seems like everyday we are fed messages of acceptance, freedom, and anything goes. When in actuality these messages, most times, pull us farther and farther from our destiny in Christ Jesus. I didn't write this book as a perfect man, but as someone who has been through the fire in some areas in my life, and found that Jesus is truly the only way. I wrote this book to let you know that the lies of the devil are not true no matter how convincing they might sound. No matter how many times he talks to you in the midnight hour telling you that you are okay, or that there's no hope for you changing, just know, he is a liar. Jesus came and gave us the keys to be free. My prayer is that you use them. I'm not saying that it won't be difficult, trying, or painful, but the thing about it is that it is necessary and well worth it. We have to change so that we might change the world.

Removing The Grave Clothes is all about us utilizing the power that God gave us when He died and rose again. We have uncovered the many areas that the devil has helped stay bound in through the book; now is time to get free from it. The first step was identifying that there is a problem, the second step is searching the Word and our past to see where the root might lay, third is repenting and asking God to help us break free, and the fourth step is an outward change that reflects and inward revelation and change. Our process is designed to help us help someone else. God didn't put you on this earth for you or allow, allow not His will for, you to go through this stuff for you. We have to get free so that we can help this generation break free of the shackles that satan has bound them with.

In closing, thank you for finishing the book and making a decision to, through your life, to make a liar and defeated foe out of the devil. I want you to know as always I'm praying for you with all supplication believing that you're doing the same for me. We are getting unwrapped from our issues together and shouting the victory as we do. Man of God, you may say that I don't know you personally, but I know the struggle of becoming God's man, so in a way we are all the same. Just know that you are an over comer and you will make it. I leave you with four words that all of us need to hear at our lowest point: I BELIEVE IN YOU!!!!!